Bluebells, Rainbows and Sheep

Bluebells, Rainbows and Sheep

A collection of poems by
DORIS SLOLEY

ryelands

First published in Great Britain in 2009

British Library Cataloguing-in-Publication Data
A CIP record for this title is available from the British Library

ISBN 978 1 906551 23 0

RYELANDS
Halsgrove House,
Ryelands Industrial Estate,
Bagley Road, Wellington, Somerset TA21 9PZ
Tel: 01823 653777   Fax: 01823 216796
email: sales@halsgrove.com

Part of the Halsgrove group of companies
Information on all Halsgrove titles is available at: www.halsgrove.com

Printed and bound by The Cromwell Press Group, Trowbridge

I dedicate this book to my parents,
Edith and Sidney Sloley,
who were both very special people.

Contents

Preface

Doris Sloley has spent her entire life on Exmoor. She was born between Wheddon Cross and Timberscombe, moved to a farm above Withypool at the age of four and now lives in the pretty village of Monksilver.

When I asked her how she would describe her own poetry, she used the word "accessible" – and this is apt. Unlike so much contemporary poetry, you don't need a key to get into Doris's poems; there is no intellectual barrier shutting out the reader. On the contrary, her poems are "hooky" – hooking you in and making you want to read on.

She paints word pictures of situations, thoughts and ideas that are recognisable to most of us, writing with an endearing gentleness, warmth, poignancy and, often, a sense of almost childlike wonderment. Her words touch a familiar chord or memory, lingering in the mind long after the book is closed.

But the sweetness and simplicity are deceptive. Like all good poets, Doris writes succinctly, consciously stringing together every carefully selected word to form an apparently effortless whole. And, after the initial quick gratification, another level of meaning is revealed, making the reader suddenly think in a different way.

This book contains poems for people of all ages to suit every kind of mood, situation and emotion. It is a book to cherish.

Jenny Glanfield

Introduction

I was nine when I composed my first poem, in bed at night before going to sleep. I never wrote it down but can still remember it now.

When I was thirteen my teacher Frances Griffin, later to become Frances Barrow, introduced us to poetry and I wrote four poems. These subsequently appeared in the school magazine. Not a smart printed publication but a rather nice, homely effort which was handwritten and held together with string.

There followed a long period when I made a few half-hearted attempts at writing but was never satisfied with any of it, as it didn't come up to Keats or Tennyson. Besides, this was at a time when writing poetry was considered very eccentric. You didn't tell anyone you wrote poetry!

By 1971, I had started writing again. First producing five poems which included "Shepherd's Song". Having always lived and worked on a farm it was inevitable that, sooner or later, I would write about my beloved sheep. My father retired from the farm in 1973 and it was a few years after this that I added the last two lines.

This was a particularly traumatic time. I took a job in an office, as a secretary and telephonist, but after three years the stress of life in the fast lane got to me and I had a nervous breakdown. This, later, gave me the inspiration for "Breakdown", which I hoped might be of some help and comfort to others in the same situation.

During 1987 and, by this time working in the surgery of the local doctors, I wrote "A Dispenser's Prayer".

The title of "The Pool by the Withys" is from the meaning of the name Withypool; the wood is Blindwell Wood on Lower Blackland Farm, where I lived for thirty-four years. We used to go to the wood, from school, for nature walks, then, as my sister, brother and I were almost there, we were allowed to go on home, which always pleased us.

"The Rat Race" came from an idea suggested to me by my sister, so she deserves at least half the credit for that one.

The fascinating differences in children, as shown to me by my four nieces, was the inspiration for "Sisters," and some unforgettable narrow boat holidays with the folk dance club led to "Away From it All".

"A Dog Called Derek" came from my, then small, neighbour Debbie's close bond with her dog.

"The Fairy Garden" was a small, rough patch of ground at the side of a neighbour's house, which two small girls, Emma and Katie, saw as a special place.

"J-Just One Last Question, Please" was from a true situation. The dustpan and brush really were tied together and, yes, it did work: they were separated soon after the poem appeared in the church magazine.

Last year I had the holiday of a lifetime, one week in Australia and four weeks in New Zealand. Sheila and Ray Bowles, my New Zealand friends, suggested I write a poem about this holiday and so "Kiwi Land" was added to my collection.

Doris Sloley – September 2009

Shepherd's Song

Your happiness is found in simple things.
Through rain and sun you're peaceful and content.
No running here and dashing there, for you.
In pastures green, life's secret you have learnt.
A wealth of worldly wisdom in your eyes;
A trust, so strong, I dare not fail to keep:
Though things may change, I know you never will.
My friends so true, my endless joy, my sheep.

Now time has flown and I am far away
Yet, still, you're there within my heart today.

13

Exmoor is...

Frosty nights and misty mornings,
Fresh green beech leaves in the spring.
Purple, heather-covered moorland,
Valleys deep where rivers sing.

Random patchwork quilts of colour,
Golden yellow, greens and browns.
Busy farmstead, homely cottage,
Sleepy village, bustling town.

Red deer, dignified and stately,
Proud, erect against the sky.
Hounds, with scarlet coated huntsmen,
Guards, protectors, standing by.

Snow which clothes the hills in silence,
Rain that clings to hair and brow.
Curve-horned sheep with kind, wise faces,
Docile, calm red-ruby cow.

Bluebell woods, rough-coated ponies,
Village shows and country rides.
Exmoor is, to me, forever,
All of these and more besides.

A Dog called Derek

I'm only just a little girl
And, sometimes, life seems hard.
There's lots of rules to keep to
When I'm playing in the yard.

But I've a very special friend.
He's with me every day.
A friend who's never mean or cross,
Who always wants to play.

My tears, they don't embarrass him.
He snuggles up to me,
With big brown eyes that soften up
In silent sympathy.

He scares away the dinosaurs
That come when I'm in bed.
They're frightened he might chew them up,
So all of them have fled.

I've entered Derek in the show.
He really is the best.
I know he'll win first prize because
He'll fight off all the rest.

My Mum and Daddy love me and
On this I can depend,
As long as I've got Derek - I
Don't need another friend.

Lock's Bazaar

I can't recall exactly where it was.
It could have been the last shop on the strand,
But to a child, of any age, it seemed
Like stepping through the door to fairyland.

Once through the door you'd stop and gaze around,
Then, nothing in the world seemed on a par
With all the wondrous treasures you beheld.
Such was the magic charm of Lock's Bazaar.

Dolls cups and plates of marbled Bakelite,
The tiny knives and forks – three pence a pair.
Some rag dolls, some of celluloid, some dressed
In comely gowns and some of them quite bare.

Buckets and spades for days on golden sands,
Tin ships to sail to lands beyond the sea.
The sweet, sharp flavour of the sherbet dips,
The scent of leather purses, drifting free.

Mouth organs, music boxes, penny flutes,
Lead soldiers to fight battles near and far.
Time had no meaning for a child like me.
Browsing for hours, spellbound, in Lock's Bazaar.

Later, when grown up things held more appeal.
The combs, bright ribbons, ornaments for hair;
The sterling silver bracelets, coloured beads;
A new excitement stirred and I would dare

To watch the owner's handsome, blond-haired son,
Who'd tidy shelves and cram a toffee jar.
The lad who filled that early teenage need
To hang around and worship from afar.

If I had chance to travel back in time,
To ride a circus horse or be a star.
The only thing I'd really want to do
Is spend another day in Lock's Bazaar.

Selina

What do you dream of, tightly curled up there,
A look of ecstasy upon your face?
Then, languidly, you stretch your limbs in bliss.
So smooth you are, epitome of grace.

Do mice, or men, make up your slumberous thoughts;
That dainty nose, a-twitch, anticipate
A banquet worthy of so fine a cat,
Or sportive jaunts beyond the farmyard gate?

My loyal friend, you are, through hope and joy:
My furry comforter in time of pain:
I do not know what mystic powers you own,
Just that I'm privileged your trust to gain.

This Land – My Land

As I walk, step by step, across this land,
Millions of years unfold before my eye
And I, in awe, begin to understand
How small a part of time I occupy.

I gaze, in wonder, at a tiny flower,
Perfectly formed by nature's skilful hand
From one small seed which multiplies to make
The fragrant beauty of a meadowland.

Rocks put together, seam on seam, through ages past,
Hewn out by sea and storm and humankind.
The valleys deep and mountains high, a gift,
A legacy that they have left behind.

Cathedrals, vast, where kings and poets lie,
Wrapped round in sleep, untouched by what they know
Of battles lost and won, and sonnets penned
Of loves forsaken, many moons ago.

Here, for what seems scarce longer than a day,
This tiny speck which I, so clearly, am
Will blossom for a while then fade away,
A minute contribution to the plan.

Taking the Biscuit

It really isn't very fair
That no-one seems to be
The slightest bit encouraging
To skinny folk, like me.

I've searched through all the magazines
And nowhere does it state
That there are tried and tested ways
To put *on* extra weight.

A size ten used to be size ten.
Now, when I buy a mac,
They call it generous sizing so
It fits me like a sack.

When I lament to chubby friends,
"It's unjust and it's sad",
They look at me as if to say,
You should be very glad.

They think I'm making fun of them,
Reproach is in their eyes.
They can't believe I'm longing to
Go up an extra size.

When I get down to two stone four
Then disappear from view,
They'll say, "She was so lucky, she
Could always eat her stew."

It, truly, takes the biscuit and
I don't know who to blame.
Someone should even out the pounds
And make us all the same.

Best Friends

I've been out here waiting for Granfer,
Oh, it must be five minutes or more.
I'm making quite sure that he sees me.
That's why I'm right here by the door.

We've played all the games I can think of,
So I thought we might go for a walk.
The very best thing about Granfers
Is - they don't seem to mind if you talk.

There might be some puddles to splash in,
So I've put on my shiny red boots.
I'm dressed for a walk in the country,
Well, you have to admit I look cute.

Dog Toby can come and chase rabbits,
And we might see some lambs or a cow.
Then, I'll pick some flowers for Mummy.
There'll be lots in the meadows, right now.

It seems like I've been here for ages,
Simply waiting for my special chum.
But I know I don't need to worry,
Because Granfer is certain to come.

For Louise

Baby with laughing eyes, you're spring;
Eager for what the years will bring.
Mum, with radiant glow, you're summer;
For you, life now holds everything.
Gran, proud adoring autumn, prays
Her pathway will be smooth and bright.
Great-Gran, winter-wise and mellow,
Knows time can make most things come right.

Sisters

One child bubbling, always full of laughter,
The other one serene and full of dreams.
One quicksilver, changing with each moment,
The other calm with quiet, gentle charm.
One a child of spring, all bright and sparkling,
The other gentle autumn, kind and sweet.
I love one the way that I love laughter.
I love the other just as I love dreams.
Each child, in her way, so very special:
Each one herself, so different, but in my eyes just the same.

Transformation

"What makes a house a home?" she asked.
And I, with hand beneath my chin,
Considering, said, "Warmth and light,
Somewhere I can be happy in.

"A table laid with homely food,
Hot buttered toast, a mug of tea,
A sanctuary when I feel sad,
Friends dropping in to chat with me.

"A purring cat beside the fire,
A dog, perhaps, to take for walks,
A jam jar crammed with daffodils,
A place where I've no need to talk.

"A child's toys strewn around the floor,
An open book, a cosy chair,
A feeling of sublime content,
In knowing all I need is there."

I scratch my head and say, "I'm sure
I've missed the most important bit."
Then realise what makes a home
Is - it must have a Mum in it.

The Culture Shock

I can cry now, I never could before.
When I moved out, and closed and locked the door
On life as it had been for all those years,
I would have cried - but numbness blocked the tears.

I watched the hammer fall on loyal friends;
Farm implements disperse to counties' ends.
I said a fond goodbye to fields and coombes,
Then walked, for one last time, through empty rooms.

The childhood haunts where once we used to play,
The picnic teas we shared when making hay:
Those memories will have to help me now
But, though I try, the way seems hard somehow.

I'm sitting here, hemmed in by walls and glass,
And I'd exchange it all for fields of grass,
Where I could wander, undisturbed and free,
With just my faithful dog for company.

January

In January, when the frost
Makes patterns on the windowpane
And Christmas candles all have gone,
The lake is frozen, once again.

In January, when the snow
Falls, thickly, on the trees and grass,
The snowdrop bows her dainty head
While people, cold and shivering, pass.

In January, best of all
The robin sings a merry tune.
He makes it known to everyone,
That spring will be a-coming soon.

Up, Up and Away

I'm flying off to distant lands
So I may be gone a while.
Will you please look after Mummy,
And be sure to make her smile.

I've been practising for ages,
And I think I've got the knack.
It's a matter now of balance
– Just a wee bit further back.

There is really nothing to it,
I shall start out very slow.
Whoops! almost tumbled off that time.
Right now, steady as I go.

There's no way of being certain
What rare treasures I shall find
When I touch down in pixie land,
And I leave the world behind.

With cities vast and castles grand,
There'll be such a lot to see,
But if I travel very fast
I might, still, be back for tea.

Return to Exmoor

Pick me a bluebell, next time you go there.
Walk through the wood and on over the stream,
Up the green slope with grasshoppers singing,
Just where I, oftentimes, go in my dreams.

I can go back, myself, if I want but
If I return to the place that I knew,
All of my memories will crowd in and then
I shall be sad - but it's different for you.

You haven't known the fun of haymaking,
Watched tadpoles wriggle and dart in the pond,
Helped to 'head out' a corn rick by moonlight,
Rode through the fields to the moorland beyond,

Run to a meadow where lambs were playing,
Skipping and racing in boundless delight,
Climbed up the hill where we would go sledging
In winter when all was coated in white.

Is there a tree, still, in the old orchard?
Can you find lanes where wild strawberries grew?
Are there blackberries, now, in the cow field?
Do you hear calls of a distant curlew?

I want to keep all these memories of mine
Locked up in my heart, unaltered by time.

The Magic Gift

If I were a fairy godmother
With a gift to bestow on a child,
I would not wish, for her, great beauty,
Nor a temperament gentle and mild.

To help her get all that she wanted
I would wish her the gift of the gab,
With words coming easily to her,
So that all the attention she'd grab.

Then she would keep people around her,
Never able to quite break away
And she would oust all competition,
For the sensitive folk would not stay.

But maybe, someday, she'd be lonely
When they tired of her trivial chat.
Nobody would want her, or love her
And, for her, I would never wish that.

So I'd wish a soul of discretion
And a heart full of kindness and care.
The words that she used would be loving.
Not so many, but measured and fair.

Then, only then, could she be happy,
Her true charm and appeal never pall.
Her face would reflect her sweet nature,
So a beauty she'd be after all.

Breakdown

I know, too well, what you are going through.
This hard, hard day is drawing to a close.
The minutes drag like never-ending years,
Caught, as you are, in nerves' relentless throes.

Now gripped by fear, no rhyme or reason why,
To rise to a crescendo, hard to bear.
Then all you ask, to crawl away and hide,
Crushed, weighted down, locked fast in deep despair.

Then night-time comes and sleep blocks out the day.
You've gained a respite 'til the morning comes.
Dawn breaks, you wake, blind panic rushes in!
Where do you find the courage to go on?

Folk shake their heads and look at you askance
But, well you know, you're just as sane as they.
In fact it's conscientious caring folk,
Like you, who always seem to get this way.

No concentration left to read or think.
This hell you can't describe compelling you
To contemplate that other, final way.
But there's one thought you have to hold fast to.

Because of those you love, and life itself,
You must press on towards hope's tiny gleam.
Although it may take time you will win through.
One day, all this will be like some bad dream.

The help that you most surely need, you find.
Then kindly words bring blessed relieving tears.
The debt you owe is a forever one,
Your shaking body calmed with pills and prayers.

And, though it's hard for you to picture now,
This tangled life will straighten out, for sure.
Your world will stabilize, then you will see
The way ahead, and you'll be whole once more.

Cavendo Tutus (safe through taking care)

"There must be peace on earth," you say,
And oh! how I agree,
But where would be the point of peace
If we could not be free.

For if a few intimidate
While others cower and cringe,
Then human dignity is lost
And human rights infringed.

In school-yard, workplace, realm or world
The principle's the same,
And meekness must be reinforced
Again, and yet again.

For nothing good comes easily,
And nothing's gained at all
If justice cannot be upheld
In causes great, or small.

When you and yours, and me and mine,
And ours and theirs agree
Then, that will be the time to say
Here's peace - guard carefully.

Tongue-tied

I can sing to you,
Say a poem too.
That's not hard to do,
I know the words, you see.

But if we should walk
And I want to talk,
It's not up in chalk:
The words must come from me.

You may think I'm brave,
Your praise you must save,
Fluency I crave
To bring you close to me.

A Dispenser's Prayer

God give, to me, the grace to be
A person of humility,
Prepared to say I may be wrong;
To help the weak; to guide the strong.

Make me unbiased, firm but kind.
Give me an ever open mind
To handle with diplomacy
The ones who share this task with me.

Give concentration all the time,
To stay my hand and guide my mind,
That no-one shall be harmed through me
And all my sleep may peaceful be.

Let me not act impatiently
With those who may much slower be,
But give them time to put their case,
For age and illness slows their pace.

And if, in anger, folk should come,
I'll try to speak in calming tone,
For faith is shaken easily
By fear and vulnerability.

People don't come in different grades.
They're all your children, by you made.
Who knows what unkind twist of fate
Has led them to their present state.

I'd like to feel that I can be
Caring, to those who trust in me;
Bring comfort in their fear and pain,
And help to make them well again.

Rainbow Days

I'm going to stitch a rainbow fine
In blues and reds and greens,
And the many shades and colours
That there are, in between.

I'll start with blue and snowy white,
The blue to match your eyes.
Then mix in golden yellow for
A beach and sunny skies.

Green will bring peace and restfulness,
Serenity and charm,
To paint the perfect picture of
A haven, safe from harm.

The silver of a baby's laugh,
And softly falling rain,
Ensuring continuity
- A never-ending chain.

There must be black for sadder days;
Of that there is no doubt.
A few fine threads, just here and there,
To make the rest stand out.

And when, at last, I've finished it,
I'll give it all to you.
Then you'll have moments filled with joy:
And days of dreams come true.

Wind of Change

There are winds from the north, and winds from the east;
There are winds from the south and the west:
Hark! now while I tell you of all of these
And the one that I love the best.

There are winds that are friends, and winds that are foes,
Always vying for space in my life,
And there's some bring peace and a quiet mind
But the others a restless strife.

There's the crash and the smash of October gales
When in fear of destruction you're caught.
Then almost as swift, it abates and brings
The sailing ship safe home to port.

Hear the softly whispering, bland summer breeze,
That stirs, gently, the trees and the grass,
And it cools and heals like a soothing balm
As it wafts, all serenely, past.

Feel the icy blast of the chill winter wind,
Cutting, keenly, through finger and toe
As, relentless, it tugs at flimsy wraps,
And piles, high, the scurrying snow.

There's a whirling, a swirling, a mad March wind
That makes the last, late brown leaves to fall.
But the soft, moist breeze of the hills and moors
Is the one I love most of all.

Tea for Two

I've washed my favourite dolly,
Dressed her in her Sunday best,
Today she's having Teddy round for tea.
I've made some cakes and jellies,
Laid the special cups and plates,
Because it is her birthday and she's three.

I've had such trouble choosing
Just what present she would like.
I thought, maybe, some ribbons or a slide.
But Teddy says she's got those,
And he thinks she'd rather have
A shaggy pony, just for her to ride.

When they had finished eating,
We weren't sure what we could do.
You can't play many games, not just with Ted.
So I've read them a story,
Then they chatted for a while.
Teddy's gone, and my dolly's tucked in bed.

Childhood Christmas

"Forty-eight, and not a word,"
That's what Mum used to say
When we children said, "What will
We get on Christmas day?"

Walls are decked with paper chains,
Holly and mistletoe.
Stir the pudding, make a wish.
Excitement starts to grow.

Christmas Eve, at last it's here,
Ash faggot in the grate,
Ginger beer for us to drink.
We mustn't stay up late.

Bumps and whispers in the night;
Pretend to be asleep:
We vowed not to look too soon,
That promise we must keep.

But temptation's strong and so
To end of bed we creep.
That torch from underneath the sheet
Alight for just one peep.

Dad calls, "Children, back to bed."
Reluctantly, we go.
Best be good or Santa may
Take all our toys, we know.

Wide awake! at break of day.
"Let's see what Santa's brought."
Paper rustling, magic sound.
"Just look at what I've got."

Now the stocking, feel the lumps.
Beads, crayons, chocolates, so
Dig right down until you find
That orange in the toe.

Run and waken Mum and Dad,
Our huge delight to share.
Spread the presents on their bed,
Content to know they care.

Off to church in sparkling frost.
There, we all sing with joy,
Hymns to celebrate the birth
Of that rare baby boy.

Home to dinner, Christmas style.
Roast goose and festive fare.
Carefully search your slice of pud.
The sixpence might be there.

Joy of loving, joy to give.
New toys, and games to play,
Praises sung and thanks bestowed.
All these make Christmas day.

The Rat Race

It's very clear, ambition
Makes the world go round.
But you can have too much of this,
As folk have often found.

You start out like a rippling stream,
Placid, calm and slow,
Then you change into a brook
With depth and even flow,

And after that a river
Going faster every day.
No time to stop for anyone
Or pass the time of day.

Then onward, ever onward
Until, just like the sea,
You keep rushing to and fro
Getting nowhere - never free.

The Rejects

I picked up a silver-framed photograph
In a charity shop, today.
It was two small children, a boy of eight
And a girl of five I would say.

They sat on a sofa and just beside,
Casting a multi-coloured glow,
Was a tiffany lamp like grandma had
When I was a child, long ago.

His bright chestnut hair slicked back from his brow,
The boy looked spruce in suit and tie.
A kind of pride in the way that he sat
With back so straight and head held high.

The girl, grey-eyed, with her blonde tumbling curls
Was a vision in midnight blue;
Legs daintily crossed at her ankles and
Displaying one fine buckled shoe.

Mixed with the saucepans and tired old clothes,
It makes me feel sad, wondering how
A picture like that could finish up there,
With no-one to treasure it now.

Well, I put it back down and turned away.
Perhaps, someday, someone will see,
Mirrored in those faces of long ago,
A face from their own family.

Away From it All

Find some green, enchanted valley,
Half forgotten by the world.
Swallows dipping, brown trout flipping,
By a tuft of grass, dew pearled.

Plough-lands red, and flower strewn meadows,
Newborn lambs with mothers mild.
Someone makes a chain of daisies,
Gives them to a little child.

Rambling hills rise up above me,
Sparkling rivers round them wind.
Ducks and drakes with downy offspring
Swim around, our scraps to find.

Trees reach down to touch the water.
Drinking, deep, from nature's store.
Pebbles, rounded by the ages,
Lie in heaps upon the shore.

Here, I dream I'll stay forever,
Not by worldly fetters bound.
In my narrow boat a-chugging,
Nowhere else such peace I've found.

Priorities

Woman, know where your power lies,
To shape the world by holding one small hand
And gently leading one small child through life's vast wonderland.
By taking time to teach him how to play and fill his time,
And pointing out, along the way, the beauty he can find.

Teach him respect for other folk
But, just as much, he must respect himself.
Give him sound rules to live by and safeguard his precious health.
Show right from wrong, give reasons why and how things should be done.
Not only once but many times, with patience and vision.

He doesn't want expensive toys
Or travel in a far exotic land,
But Mum, close by, to guide him when he needs a helping hand,
Who'll dry his tears, bandage his knee and calm his troubled mind,
And show the worth of justice in his dealings with mankind.

Better, by far, you spend your time
In showing him that he is quite secure,
Giving encouragement and a faith in himself that is sure,
Than striving, resolutely, to accomplish change worldwide,
Or building empty achievements for short-lived, personal pride.

You have a sacred trust in life;
A torch to hold; a very special plan:
The values that you give this child will far outreach your span,
And you will understand, in time, as history's unfurled,
That the hand that rocks the cradle does, truly, rule the world.

Trash or Treasure

I think I'll tidy out a drawer
And throw some stuff away.
There must be lots of things in here
I don't need, anyway.

There on the top, beyond repair,
The necklace you gave me,
Two seashells, an elastic band
And one redundant key.

Then, further down, some kitchen string;
A brooch without a pin;
Old programmes from a pantomime
Someone I know was in.

A tatty photo of a dog,
Much loved but gone away;
A handmade spray of flowers I wore
On someone's wedding day.

A button from a uniform;
A badge with outspread wings,
Three paper clips, some foreign stamps,
Two wooden curtain rings.

Attachments for the garden hose
But no-one told me how.
Pink buttons from a baby-coat.
She doesn't need it now.

A button hook, for leggings my
Dad wore around the farm.
A badge with "3 today" on and
A single lucky charm.

A pink designer lipstick which
I've hardly used at all;
A comb with one tooth missing and
A mitten, much too small.

I find an empty scent bottle
And hold it to my nose.
It's funny, how I think of you
Each time I smell 'Black Rose'.

This piece of quartz from sandy shores
Has, long since, lost its sheen.
And deep beneath it all, there lurks
One lonely runner bean.

Now that I've finished sorting through,
It seems a whole lot more.
I've plumped up all the clutter and
I just can't close the drawer.

Please, don't throw out a memory.
You might need it one day,
To chase away the winter blues
And cheer you on your way.

J-just One Last Question Please

I'm no longer on the church council
So, on matters at issue, I'll hush.
But the one thing I wanted to ask, is
Why the dustpan is tied to the brush.

Did somebody think we might nick it?
(I've a perfectly good one at home)
'Sides it hasn't got legs or four wheels on
So it's very unlikely to roam.

I'm doing my thrice yearly duty
Placing flowers, and cleaning and such.
With the floral arrangements completed
I can get down to cleaning the church.

There's plenty to do at the weekend
So I'm usually in a fair rush,
But the part that makes me feel frustrated
Is the dustpan being tied to the brush.

A large pile of dirt I've collected.
I reach the brush out for some more.
With a flip-flop the dustpan turns over
And the jolly lot lands on the floor.

I've gathered the fluff at the altar,
Round the back of the chair there's still some.
Then I find, to my immense annoyance,
The brush goes - but the dustpan won't come.

Are there ways I can get my point over?
Do I have to come right out and beg?
I'm beginning to get a bit cross now,
'Cause I've got the string wound round my leg.

It isn't the place for bad language.
It would bring down the heavenly wrath.
But, the truth is that this situation
Would try, even, a man of the cloth.

You may ask why don't I untie it.
Rules are rules! so temptation I'll crush.
I'd feel guilty if someone should catch me,
So the dustpan stays tied to the brush.

Compliment – or Not

It was all a long, long time ago
And I've no regrets, not now.
But did you have to give my name to
Your pedigree Friesian cow?

Just Desserts

They strolled, together, round the yard;
Darby and Joan, the perfect pair.
He guarded her by night and day
And all their corn and mash they'd share.

But time went by and Darby changed,
He turned on Joan, so soft and meek.
He bullied her and beat her up,
And tweaked her feathers with his beak.

Things went from bad to worse and then
It, very soon, came to the crunch.
Because he treated Joan so bad
We dined on Darby for our lunch.

Now Joan walks free, and safe from harm.
She's happier without her friend.
But Darby was so very tough,
He had the last laugh in the end.

The Fairy Garden

Tiptoe through the Fairy Garden.
Glance around, but have a care.
Never speak above a whisper
Lest you wake the fairies there.

Dusk will find them busy sewing
Gossamer to make a gown.
Wielding daisies for umbrellas
When the rain is tumbling down.

Late at night and they'll be dancing
By the lake, beneath the trees.
Tripping lightly in the moonlight;
Floating on a summer breeze.

If you're lucky you might see them
Drink fresh dew from buttercups;
Listen to their merry laughter
While on fairy bread they sup.

You won't find them in the daytime.
Best to go at close of day.
Only special, little people
Join the fairies at their play.

54

Keepsakes

How can I bear the past?
Glimpses of some forgotten, far off, days
Tug at my heart when autumn leaves shake down,
Then steal away, and vanish in the haze.

Stray thoughts of golden hours
Come, bitter-sweet, like some obscure refrain
Made precious by the transience of time,
And fill my eyes with tears I can't explain.

Still summer nights glow red
And morning mists go hunting from the stream.
Stray shadows slide across my windowpane,
Just out of reach, like memories of a dream.

Old friends, old loves, return.
Sadness and joy become as one, somehow.
Fresh as today are yesterdays long gone.
The might-have-beens that never will be now.

Twinkle

She's black and white with big green eyes
And bright as she can be,
And though she's just a kitten-cat,
I know that she loves me.

She has a sleek and shiny coat
- The very softest fur,
She'll rub her head against my arm,
Then cuddle up, and purr.

She's there to meet me, at the door
When I come home each day.
She likes to trot along with me
And join me at my play.

My kitten is my pride and joy,
The prettiest in town.
I'll always take good care of her
And never let her down.

56

The Bikers

We're a pair of dirt bike riders,
I'm steering and my mate's on the back.
We're out to stick a move on the rest
- Tear it up at the head of the pack.

Can you picture the elation,
On two wheels with the wind in your face.
Just battling it out with the big boys,
We're the guys who are setting the pace.

I like being a bare foot rider,
It's so cool and it gives me more bite.
We'll be right up there with the action
When we're burning the rubber tonight.

We're the new hope for Motocross.
Undeniably, we've got the speed.
We'll make the most of the glory days
With the two of us sharing the lead.

The Pool by the Withys

There was a wood
Which once I knew
Where, underneath the withy trees,
The bluebells grew.

A carpet rare,
With perfume sweet.
A drifting stretch of azure blue
Around my feet.

Soft mossy banks
Of deepest green.
The river pools where tawny trout
Were often seen.

The bracken tall
Where rabbits played.
That fallen tree where dreams were shared
And plans were made.

And sometimes, now,
When days come fair,
High in the tree a blackbird sings
Then - I am there.

Rainbow's End

You're the tick of the clock in the corner;
You're the candle I light when it's dark;
A good book I read over and over;
And the pure, argent song of the lark.

You're my first cup of tea in the morning;
You're the perfume of newly made hay;
Fresh cream on my bread, with strawberry jam;
And my wine at the end of the day.

You're the rustle of leaves in the autumn;
You're the first tiny snowdrop of spring;
The bright sparkle of frost in the winter;
And warm breezes that summer days bring.

You're a symphony without an ending;
Dancing firelight, soft lamplight and snow;
You're my Santa Claus and the tooth fairy;
Woolly mittens when cold east winds blow.

You're the gold at the end of the rainbow;
You're my sweetest of dreams when I sleep;
Star of Venus to guard me and guide me;
Precious treasure to cherish - and keep.

If You've Got it – Flaunt it!

I thought, perhaps, you'd like to take my photo.
I really am quite beautiful, you see.
I don't want you to think that I'm a poser.
It's plain to all, that I am quality.

I always said that I could be a model,
It's just a case of who you know, my dear.
If you've got what it takes, it's very easy.
I've got the figure and the looks, that's clear.

Nobody ever likes to share the limelight
And, maybe, all my friends will think I'm mean,
But I'll stand here then you can get a close-up.
I show up rather well against the green.

I thought I might take this a little further.
There's lots of openings for a girl like me.
But I don't want to leave my lovely meadow.
This is my home - it's where I want to be.

Homemaker

Create a world within four walls,
A haven fair, where I can go
When all the world outside looms large
And cares and worries overflow.

This cottage small, with cosy rooms,
Which shelters me when days are bleak,
Holds all the comfort that I need
And all the happiness I seek.

It beckons me when, far from home,
Keen pangs of longing tug like pain.
I hurry, hurry 'til at last
I'm cradled 'twixt its walls again.

And if you chance to pass this way
You'll feel it reaching out to you,
With gentle warmth, to breathe fresh life
And send you forth restored anew.

Kiwi Land

In a far-flung land there's a traveller
And I can't believe that it's me.
I'm standing here 'neath a sapphire sky
Where Kapiti coast meets the sea.

Fiery skies on a late spring evening,
Rainbow shells on a nearby shore,
Punga fern or the nikau palm tree:
Wonders I've never seen before.

Snow-capped mountains above green valleys,
Sleepy lagoons and waterfalls.
Cities, where houses cling to hillsides,
Bushland, dense, where the kiwi calls.

Tuatara, primeval reptile,
Guardian of knowledge, from afar,
Creature of Maori myth and legend,
Guiding spirits back to the stars.

Tree-clad cliffs, fringed by golden beaches;
Perfect peace, away from the crowd:
Upside down, at the end of the world
In the land of the long white cloud.

Acknowledgements

My grateful thanks to Jenny Glanfield for her encouragement, her tireless efforts in helping me put my book together and for the wonderful things she has done with my photographs to form the illustrations. My thanks, also, to my sister Rita, my brother Ernest and their families for allowing me to raid their photographs and for giving me the inspiration for some of the poems. To Sheila and Ray Bowles for giving me the idea for the design of the book. To Andrew and Christine Howe for the loan of the photograph for "A Dog called Derek". Also to Joan Astell for kindly allowing me to use her photograph of Lock's Bazaar from her book *Around Minehead*. My thanks to Tony Gibson for the beautiful cover photograph and to my nephew Graham for agreeing to appear on it with his sheep. Finally, I would like to mention Sheelagh, Anne, Bert and Norma, also Gail, who is sadly no longer with us. They have all been very generous with their encouragement and praise and that has meant a lot to me.

Three of these poems - "Shepherd's Song", "This Land - My Land" and "Homemaker" first appeared in *Evergreen* magazine. "Exmoor is…" appeared in *The Exmoor Review* and *visitdunster.co.uk* are using it on their website. "A Dispenser's Prayer", "Breakdown", "Priorities" and "The Rat Race" were published in *The Journal of the Dispensing Doctors' Association*.